ANNA STRONG

A Spy During the American Revolution

written by
Sarah Glenn Marsh

illustrated by
Sarah Green

Abrams Books for Young Readers • New York

General George Washington was worried about America.

He had led the Continental Army to victory in Boston two years ago, but he had lost several battles since. Many of his men were hungry, injured, or sick. The future looked dark for his young country.

One cold night in early 1778, as General Washington huddled in his tent, he wondered how he could turn the war around. Without knowing the British army's every move, America would surely lose its fight for freedom.

As the general's eyelids grew heavy, the answer came to him: America needed *spies*!

George asked his friend Major Benjamin Tallmadge to form and oversee a new group of spies called the Culper Ring. General Washington had taken the name from Culpeper, Virginia, a place he'd worked as a boy.

Major Tallmadge devised a special code so spies could pass messages that the British could not read. But even with the code and brave men fighting for the country behind the scenes, America wasn't close to winning the war. The spies who infiltrated British officers' meetings to learn valuable information were sometimes caught, and every arrest hurt America's chance for victory.

It was time to get help from someone new . . . someone different.

Major Tallmadge knew just who . . . a woman!

Anna Smith Strong!

Anna lived in Setauket on Long Island, near the British headquarters in New York City. It would be a great place for spying.

Her relatives were Loyalists, supporters of the British, which meant no one would suspect Anna of helping America. Anna was well placed to be a successful spy. She was at ease around other people and attended British society parties in New York City, while dreaming of the day when America, the land she loved and grew up in, would be free.

Anna was the last person anyone would dare accuse of being a spy.

And when Major Tallmadge asked her to become one for her beloved country, she agreed.

Anna's husband, Selah, an American soldier, also became a spy. It was a dangerous job for them both that could end in capture, prison, and even death.

But Anna wasn't afraid. She compared it to when she was a girl listening outside her mother's parlor for the latest gossip, only far more important.

Anna was proud to be part of this courageous group of patriots, especially since she was the only woman among them. She hoped that would change in time.

94: Courage

Major Tallmadge warned Anna that the British might shoot a spy on sight—even one in petticoats.

Two years earlier, a spy named Nathan Hale had been hanged without a trial for being an American spy, and the risks were just as high now.

One of her first missions was to accompany her neighbor and fellow spy, Abraham Woodhull, to New York City to gather information on the British army. Anna pretended to be Abraham's wife, and they made up a story about visiting relatives in the city, which wasn't totally false. Anna's brothers lived in Manhattan, and since they were Loyalists, she hoped to learn information about the British from them. She also bought cloth and dry goods, making it seem like she really was there to enjoy the city.

Enemy soldiers might have suspected Abraham and detained him for questioning if he was on his own, but with the charming Anna by his side, they made it safely to New York City and back.

175:
Enemy

Anna kept her spy activities well hidden, and the other spies took care to keep her work for the Culper Ring a secret, too. Once, a spy named Caleb Brewster was waiting in Anna's garden to have a private meeting with another spy. While waiting, a British officer passed by Caleb's hiding spot!

Caleb could have captured or killed the soldier, but he didn't want to draw suspicion to Anna. She would have been questioned by British authorities about the incident since Caleb was in *her* garden. The incident passed without anyone being discovered.

**31:
Arrest**

Anna's husband, Selah, wasn't as lucky. Shortly after they started spying, he was arrested for "covertly sending messages to the enemy."

British soldiers locked him up on a prison ship named *Jersey*, and a fellow spy hurried to bring word to Anna.

Other spies told her that the living conditions on the prison ship were horrible. It was overrun with rats and there was little to eat. She would have to act quickly to save Selah's life.

489: Prison

Anna couldn't risk revealing herself as a spy, not with her children depending on her, but she also couldn't abandon Selah.

She kept making trips to New York City with Abraham, hoping to learn more about the British army's plans, and on every visit, she saw the prison ship bobbing in the harbor.

She knew Selah was there, miserable and waiting for her. Counting on her help.

402:
Miserable

Anna also continued helping the other spies pass messages—often written in invisible ink and in Major Tallmadge's special code—on a long route across the waters of the Long Island Sound.

All the while, she was thinking of ways to get onto the heavily guarded prison ship. She couldn't swim there, and she was too small to wear a British soldier's uniform.

Suddenly, she had an idea. A simple one: She would bribe her way on board!

And the bribe worked! The British soldiers let her on board the *Jersey* to visit Selah. The meals she brought him on her trips to the city kept him alive until she convinced her Loyalist relatives to have him and their children moved to a safe house in Connecticut, far from British eyes.

One day British officers came knocking at her door, demanding that Anna let them occupy her family's beautiful manor home as a new headquarters.

Anna gathered up her favorite belongings. She wouldn't go far, not when she could spy on the British right from her family's land. While the soldiers had their backs turned, she hid her silver and moved into a small cottage. From there, she would make sure the enemies didn't ruin the home her ancestors worked so hard to build. More important, she could eavesdrop and learn what the soldiers were planning.

She'd just have to be very careful.

Major Tallmadge gave Anna the responsibility to signal another spy when there was a message ready to be passed. It would be carried along a complicated route across the Long Island Sound to Connecticut, then on to General Washington's headquarters.

At first, Anna thought about using a lantern, but then she had a better idea . . .

Anna hung a dripping black petticoat on her clothesline.

The British never suspected a woman's clothes hanging outside meant a message was ready to be delivered to General Washington.

Soon, Anna figured out more ways she could use her linens to pass messages to the other spies.

Handkerchiefs on her clothes line told the location of a boat hidden in a nearby cove. If there were four, Major Tallmadge and the others knew to check a certain cove. If there were six, they'd check another.

The British officers often strolled past Anna's cottage, as she hung out her petticoats. What if they realized what she was doing and locked her up on the *Jersey*?

But she couldn't be afraid. America needed her.

One night, another spy came to visit Anna with a very important message about where the British army would be moving next.

Anna knew what this meant: a chance for America to get a step ahead of the British and finally start winning the war for their freedom. Now it was up to her to signal to a third spy who would take the message across the sound to General Washington.

Early the next morning, Anna grabbed her laundry basket and hurried outside. She could feel the eyes of the soldiers on her, but she never gave them a reason to suspect her. She hung handkerchiefs and petticoats in neat rows, like she did every day.

There was nothing she could do now but sit by her window, watching the British soldiers, and wait. Anna hoped that General Washington would get the message.

And he did.

Washington used the secrets Anna and the Culper Ring spies passed him to anticipate enemy troops' movements and plan ahead, helping to win the Battle of Yorktown.

659: Victory

And eventually, the ultimate victory.

Independence!

422:
Nation

When the good news reached Anna, she celebrated with her family. By that time, Selah and their children had returned home.

Anna knew that some people were worried about the future of their young nation, but she wasn't afraid. She was glad she'd risked her life for her family's and her nation's new freedoms.

And *President* George Washington was glad his spies had trusted the clever Anna Strong. She was just the woman America needed.

THE CULPER RING CODE BOOK

The Culper Spy Ring developed a code for the letters they wrote to General George Washington, in case their messages were seized by the British. Each number stood for a word or the name of one of the spies. These messages were often written in invisible ink, which was a mixture of ferrous sulfate (a green iron salt) and water. Nicknamed "sympathetic stain," this ink was invented by physician James Jay before the war. To reveal the hidden words, a recipient would place the message over a candle flame or apply a chemical like sodium carbonate.

WRITE YOUR OWN SECRET MESSAGES!

Use the Culper Code and invisible ink.

Here are some words to get you started:

agent: **23**

alarm: **39**

ally: **25**

arrest: **31**

attack: **38**

better: **60**

bring: **54**

British: **72**

captain: **86**

careful: **87**

city: **88**

confident: **111**

Congress: **85**

courage: **94**

danger: **132**

deceive: **144**

deliver: **156**

disagree: **150**

enemy: **175**

England: **745**

faithful: **199**

farm: **184**

favor: **200**

foggy: **196**

friend: **188**

General George Washington: **711**

gentleman: **237**

gloomy: **226**

gold: **223**

grateful: **233**

guide: **222**

happy: **257**

hope: **253**

horse: **255**

human: **262**

important: **317**

impress: **290**

invite: **303**

John Bolton: **721** (code name for Major Benjamin Tallmadge, Washington's head spy)

lady: **355** (While it's not known if Anna had a code name, 355 was a code word that may have referred to her because she was a lady working with Tallmadge and his partners.)

Long Island: **723**

memorial: **406**

miserable: **402**

nation: **422**

occupy: **451**

party: **479**

people: **486**

please: **475**

pretend: **503**

prison: **489**

promise: **491**

reader: **552**

Samuel Culper: **722** (code name for Anna's neighbor, Abraham Woodhull)

secret: **596**

summer: **605**

surprise: **604**

tyranny: **646**

victory: **659**

visit: **657**

war: **680**

You can find the complete code list and more information about the code at this website: www.mountvernon.org/george-washington/the-revolutionary-war/spying-and-espionage/the-culper-code-book.

Invisible Ink

INGREDIENTS AND TOOLS

- Water
- Baking soda
- Measuring cup
- Cotton swabs or paintbrush
- White paper
- Dark juice such as grape juice

DIRECTIONS

1. Mix equal parts water and baking soda in the measuring cup.
2. Dip a cotton swab or paintbrush into the baking soda mixture "ink" to write a message on the white paper.
3. Let the ink dry thoroughly.
4. Give the message to its intended recipient (a fellow spy for instance).
5. To read the message, paint over the paper—using another cotton swab or the paintbrush—with purple grape juice. The message will appear!

AUTHOR'S NOTE

Anna Smith Strong (1740–1812), who often went by "Nancy," was born in Setauket, New York, on April 14, 1740. Her great-grandparents were some of the first English settlers in the Long Island area. She grew up in the manor her great-grandfather had built upon arriving in the colonies. At age twenty, Anna married soldier and patriot Selah Strong, and she continued living in her family's manor with him.

While there is no clear documentation that Anna was, in fact, a spy for the Culper Ring, there is plenty of evidence to *suggest* that she was. For instance, she made at least one documented trip to New York City with her neighbor Abraham Woodhull during the war. There are also mentions of the Strong family's home and property in surviving letters written by Culper members, and there is even a vague reference to Anna in British wartime correspondence. It comes from British spy William Heron, who wrote to Oliver DeLancey, British intelligence chief, on Long Island, on February 4, 1781: "Private dispatches are frequently sent from your city to the Chieftain [Washington] here by some traitors. They come by the way of Setalket [sic], where a certain Brewster receives them at, or near, a certain woman's."

It is documented that Anna was friends with Caleb Brewster and Abraham Woodhull, two known Culper spies; it's also documented that Brewster once hid from the British in the Strong family's backyard. After Selah was released to patriot-occupied Connecticut, Anna appears to have remained on her family's land, allowing her to keep an eye on their property throughout the remainder of the war. It also positioned her perfectly to assist the Setauket spies. The story about Anna using her laundry line and petticoats to help pass messages and signal the location of boats has remained a part of Setauket's folklore and family tradition to this day.

There is also a primary source that historians often point to when arguing that Anna was a spy for the Culper Ring: the use of the code word 355, meaning "lady," in a letter from Abraham Woodhull to Major Tallmadge on August 15, 1779. It read, "I intend to visit 727 [New York] before long and think by the assistance of a 355 [lady] of my acquaintance, shall be able to outwit them all." Many believe "355" refers to Anna, because as the wife of known patriot and rebel Selah Strong and the neighbor and friend of Abraham Woodhull, Anna was uniquely positioned to assist her fledgling country. Historians further believe that so little is written about her involvement with the Culper Ring because of the vigilant steps taken to protect her identity.

President George Washington himself visited the Strong family at their home following the war, also visiting known Culper spies Brewster and Woodhull. Some historians point to this visit as further proof of Anna's involvement in the Culper Ring activities, as it would have taken significant contributions to the war to prompt a special postwar visit from the very busy Washington.

After the war, Anna and Selah had another son, in 1783, and named him George Washington Strong—further evidence of Anna's loyalty to America. It remains a mystery why Anna was so patriotic when she had many relatives who wanted the colonies to remain part of England. Perhaps she was inspired by her husband, friends, and neighbors who spied for America at such great risk to themselves. Or perhaps Anna simply knew that a free America would be a wonderful place to live.

ARTIST'S NOTE

As this is a book about American history, I wanted to make sure that there was accuracy in my period references but also keep the illustrations within my own style. I looked at the art of John Trumbull and Emanuel Gottlieb Leutze for their sense of motion and action, eighteenth-century etchings and watercolors for palette inspiration and linework, and many online resources, particularly the Metropolitan Museum of Art Costume Institute's search engine.

To play with the spy element, I used more framed spots than I would normally do in a picture book, providing a "spyglass" effect where we're zooming in on the action and letting the reader be in on the secret. In a similar vein, I gave Anna a different floral dress in every picture because I wanted to explore themes of camouflage—but her strength is that she hid in plain sight. I wanted her to blend with innocuous things that are all around but that you may not pay much attention to. At the same time, the flowers still stand out. I also included floral patterns in a lot of the backgrounds so that Anna would both blend in and be noticeable. Anna's overall look is also meant to be one of a sort of "contained" adventurous attitude, with her curls and loose hairstyle: I wanted her to look a bit rebellious in comparison to the other women. I loved the opportunity to bring Anna's story to life, to let it be known that women, too, were in the forefront of the American Revolution.

NOTES

Page 11: One of her first missions . . . enjoy the city: Alexander Rose, *Washington's Spies*, 173.

Page 12: Once, a spy named Caleb Brewster . . . discovered: Alexander Rose, *Washington's Spies*, 234.

Page 23: The British never suspected a woman's clothes: Lisa Tendrich Frank, *An Encyclopedia of American Women at War*, 522.

Page 36: "Private dispatches are frequently sent . . . a certain woman's": Beverly Tyler, "A Case for Anna Smith Strong," 4.

Page 36: "I intend to visit 727 . . . outwit them all": Beverly Tyler, "A Case for Anna Smith Strong," 2.

SELECTED BIBLIOGRAPHY

Baker, Mark Allen. *Spies of Revolutionary Connecticut: From Benedict Arnold to Nathan Hale*. Charleston, SC: The History Press, 2014.

Frank, Lisa Tendrich. *An Encyclopedia of American Women at War: From the Home Front to the Battlefields*. Santa Barbara, CA: ABC-CLIO, 2013.

"George Washington, Spymaster." *George Washington's Mount Vernon*. www.mountvernon.org/george-washington/the-revolutionary-war/spying-and-espionage/george-washington-spymaster/.

Hunter, Ryan Ann. *In Disguise!: Undercover with Real Women Spies*. New York: Simon and Schuster, 2013.

Rose, Alexander. *Washington's Spies: The Story of America's First Spy Ring*. New York: Bantam Dell, 2006.

Tyler, Beverly. "A Case for Anna Smith Strong: Her Relationship with the Setauket-Based Culper Spy Ring." Three Village Historical Society. www.threevillagehistoricalsociety.org.

ACKNOWLEDGMENTS

This book wouldn't have been possible without Christa Heschke's belief in it from day one and the guidance of my editor, Howard Reeves, who brought out the best in this story. I'd like to thank the whole team at Abrams Kids, as well as my husband Chris, who listened to many drafts. Lastly, I'd like to remember my ancestor, Benjamin Pendleton, a great-grandfather several times removed and a soldier in the Revolutionary War, and all those who fought for America.

—S.G.M.

INDEX

To my mom, Cathy, the bravest,
strongest woman I know.
—S.G.M.

To my family, who have always encouraged
me to reach my goals. I wouldn't be anywhere
without your love and support.
And to all the women of history, secret and
known, who paved the way for people like me.
I hope to get to keep telling your stories.
—S.G.

The illustrations in this book were made using Photoshop.
Cataloging-in-Publication Data has been applied for and may be obtained from the Library of Congress.
ISBN 978-1-4197-3419-9

Text copyright © 2020 Sarah Glenn Marsh
Illustrations copyright © 2020 Sarah Green
Edited by Howard W. Reeves
Book design by Steph Stilwell

Printed and bound in China
10 9 8 7 6 5 4 3 2 1

Abrams Books for Young Readers are available at special discounts when purchased in
quantity for premiums and promotions as well as fundraising or educational use. Special editions can also be
created to specification. For details, contact specialsales@abramsbooks.com or the address below.

Abrams® is a registered trademark of Harry N. Abrams, Inc.

ABRAMS The Art of Books
195 Broadway, New York, NY 10007
abramsbooks.com